The Zen Habits
Beginner's Guide to Mindfulness

The Zen Habits
Beginner's Guide to Mindfulness

*Learn the fundamental skill
for habit change and happiness*

Leo Babauta

Waking Lion Press

Dedicated to my readers who are struggling. I love you deeply.

ISBN 978-1-4341-0521-9

This book is uncopyrighted. The author and publisher release all rights to the work contained herein. Freely use the text as you like.

Published by Waking Lion Press, an imprint of the Editorium

Waking Lion Press™ and Editorium™ are trademarks of:

The Editorium, LLC
West Jordan, UT 84081-6132
www.editorium.com

The views expressed in this book are the responsibility of the author and do not necessarily represent the position of Waking Lion Press. The reader alone is responsible for the use of any ideas or information provided by this book.

Contents

	Introduction: What You'll Get Out of This Book	vii
1	The Honest Truth	1
2	The Start — How to Meditate	4
3	The 15 Problems You'll Face	9
4	How to Progress	16
5	Working with Your Struggle	20
6	Why We Struggle	24
7	The Heart of the Struggle Is Groundlessness	29
8	Staying with Curiosity and Compassion	34
9	How to Not Cling	38
10	Developing Patience	41

11	Dealing with Overwhelm	44
12	Changing Habits	47
13	Finding Focus	52
14	How to Get Better	55

About the Author 59

Introduction: What You'll Get Out of This Book

This isn't a book about how to find peace, calm and Zen — though you might reach those places at times with the methods in this book.

This isn't a book about always living life in the moment. Being present is a part of the mindfulness training we'll do here, but there isn't goal to live in the present all the time. I haven't found that to be possible, though when I do achieve it, it's excellent.

This is a book about training your mind. And shifting your focus. And dealing with struggles. And changing your habits.

I've found mindfulness to be the key to changing everything in your life. That might seem trite, but consider my findings through years and years of working with my own habit changes and many other peoples' as well:

1. Lots of people struggle to change habits even if

they know what steps to take. The reason is because of patterns of thinking that are sabotaging them, that they aren't aware of.

2. We all struggle with distractions and procrastination. Why? Because of fears and habitual mental patterns that keep us stuck on distractions and turning us from focus. We are unaware of these fears and mental patterns as well.

3. We all struggle with stress, frustration, feeling bad about ourselves, disliking situations we're in, unhappiness with other people. Why? Because of certain ideals that we're clinging to. Letting go of these attachments is the solution, but without awareness of what's going on, we can't let go.

4. We often struggle with finances and clutter, based on habits of procrastination and urges to buy stuff on impulse. There's a lot to these ideas, but I'll ask you to trust me on this as I don't have space to cover this in detail. The problem is that the procrastination and urges are happening in the background, and we can't deal with them if we're not aware of them.

I could go on, but you can see the problem: we're not aware of the things that are causing our problems. Developing an awareness through the mental training of mindfulness is the answer. It helps you change everything, much more than almost anyone realizes.

Introduction: What You'll Get Out of This Book

So I'm not going to help you fix all these problems in one book. That would be a series of books or courses, which I hope to develop eventually. Today, we're going to work on a set of skills that will enable the fixes to all these problems.

Here's what we'll be working on:

1. Mindfulness training. Basically, training ourselves to focus and stay with what we find in our minds and bodies.

2. Courage training. We normally try to avoid the things that arise, but we're going to develop the courage to stay with them. This takes practice, and you'll want to put this off, run to distractions, or use various methods to feel you have control over things that come up. Instead, we'll just focus on staying.

3. Self-compassion training. There will be difficulties that arise as we train our minds to stay. We can try to ignore them, try to push them away, try to talk ourselves out of the difficulties. But the best method, I've found, is to give compassion to these difficulties, like a good friend would if you were struggling. We'll train ourselves to do this, and it will work wonders if we do.

4. Applying these skills to problem areas. We all have areas we struggle with — whether this is frustration, feeling down, stress, struggling with habits, difficulties with other people, feeling bad

about ourselves. We'll learn to apply the skills we're learning to all these areas.

Those are a lot of important things to work on! But we'll do it in small doses, a little each day, and you'll be amazed at the progress if you stick with it for awhile.

This is going to be a purposefully short book — I want you to be able to read a chapter in a short sitting, and then put it into practice. In fact, you might be able to read the entire book in one sitting, but I recommend that you do a chapter a day for about two weeks.

I ask you to trust me. I know some of you are skeptical, and that's OK. Try it and see if I am full of it. If I'm wrong, you wasted some time but learned that I'm full of it. If I'm right, you've learned some extremely valuable life skills.

I know some of you might still have ideals about living the peaceful Zen life of mindfulness and being present all the time. You might have ideas that meditating will bring you calm. You'll likely be disabused of those notions once you get started, because this kind of training can be a bit of a struggle. That's OK — struggle is what we're learning to deal with! We want to struggle, and get good at handling it.

Trust me, and trust yourself to do the training with joy and courage and love.

Let's get started!

Chapter 1

The Honest Truth

A lot of people will try to sell you a fantasy: do the steps in this book at it will change your life! You'll be peaceful and calm and mindful and life will be amazing!

I'm not that kind of writer. I'm going to give you the honest truth, because otherwise, when you start this training, you'll be severely disappointed. If you are, you'll probably blame yourself instead of me, but honestly it's my fault if I gave you the wrong idea when you get started.

Here's the honest truth about mindfulness:

- It's hard
- It's messy
- It involves lots of failure
- You have to push into discomfort
- It will often pull rug out from under your feet

- It takes lots of practice
- It takes years to get good at it
- You forget a lot
- You think you're doing it wrong
- It'll show you that you're not as disciplined as you think
- Just when you think you know what you're doing, you're asked to go deeper
- When you think other people should be more mindful, you're wrong
- It requires love

Whew! That's a lot of honesty. In fact, some of you might be discouraged from even starting. Don't be! Here's what you'll also find:

- You just need to take small steps
- You'll progress gradually, and even a little progression can make a big difference
- It's worth the struggle and practice
- It can help you develop better relationships (with others and yourself)
- It'll help you get better at habits

- You can get better at focus and overcoming procrastination
- You don't need to be that disciplined — you just need to have the courage to keep coming back

I won't sell you a fantasy, but I can tell you that it has changed my life more than almost anything else I've learned and practiced. I am not "good" at mindfulness, nor am I that disciplined about it. I just keep coming back, and keep learning new things.

Let's get started, my friends. We'll struggle, we'll learn, we'll enjoy the journey together.

Exercise

Reflect on what ideals you have about mindfulness at the moment. What fears do you have? What is coming up in you that makes you want to avoid it, procrastinate? There are no right answers, and whatever you come up with is OK. Just take a moment to reflect on these questions.

Chapter 2

THE START — HOW TO MEDITATE

The basic practice of this book is sitting meditation. Don't worry, it's not complicated or very difficult to learn. That doesn't mean it's easy, but you can do it every day, anywhere, with no special equipment or environment.

The Setup

All you need is a place to sit. You can sit anywhere: on a chair, on a couch, on your bed, on a meditation cushion. You don't need a special cushion to do this.

It's great if you have a quiet place where you won't get interrupted. Don't get stuck on this — you don't need absolute quiet (in fact, you won't find it), and getting interrupted isn't that big of a deal. When my family interrupts my meditation, I try to smile and say hello.

If you can find a quiet place, though, that's good. It might be your living room, your bedroom, the bathroom, your backyard, a nearby park, your desk, or your commute on the train or bus. If you have a phone or stopwatch, it's useful to set a timer. Not necessary, but I do recommend it if you have the equipment. You don't need a special meditation app.

The Method of Body Awareness

So you'll want to sit comfortably to get started. Awareness of your body is how you start, so as you get started, notice these cues:

1. How are your feet? If you're sitting on a chair or couch, have your feet flat on the ground if possible. If you're sitting on a cushion, look up the lotus or half lotus position, or if you're like me, look up the Burmese position. Feel the ground beneath your feet, whatever position you're in.

2. How is your torso? Have your torso upright, with your shoulders and spine and hips all lined up. Straighten your spine by pulling the top of your head towards the ceiling, then relaxing just a tiny bit so you're not stiff. Lean forward a little bit, but don't hunch forward.

3. Notice your head. Align your ears with your

shoulders and hips. Let your jaw relax instead of clenching. Keep your mouth closed but your teeth slightly apart. Keep your tongue lightly touching the back of your front upper teeth.

4. Notice your arms and hands. Keep your arms hanging comfortably at your side, your hands can relax on your lap wherever you feel comfortable.

5. Now do a scan of your body, noticing where there's tension. Try tensing your muscles in a tense body part, then relaxing them.

You don't have to get all this perfect at first. It's not important, but come back to these instructions regularly to learn the cues gradually.

The Method of Breath Awareness

Once you've positioned your body and practiced awareness with it, we'll go to basic breath meditation. This is something you can practice for years, and even as we get into other things you can practice during sitting meditation (in later chapters), you can always start with breath meditation.

Here's how it works:

1. Put the fingertip of your attention on your breath. I like to put it in the area of my upper chest where I can feel the breath entering and leaving, but you

can also choose the entrances of your nostrils or the back of your throat. It doesn't matter much.

2. Keep your attention on your breath as it enters and exits your body.

3. It is helpful to count the breaths: one on inbreath, no count on outbreath, two on inbreath, and so on until you get to 10. Start again at one.

4. When (not if) your mind wanders just notice and gently bring your attention back to the breath. Start back at one. No need to be harsh on yourself, this returning your attention is part of the training. Be gentle and kind.

5. It can be helpful, when your mind wanders to some train of thought, to label your thinking as "thinking." Just label it and return to your breath.

That's it! Just stay on the breath, count your breaths, return gently when your mind wanders. Label your thinking and come back, again and again.

You will likely find this to be a struggle. Your mind will wander many times. That's OK. It's supposed to be a bit of a struggle, and you are supposed to learn to notice your mind wandering and to return gently and with compassion.

Your mind might even wander for the entire meditation. That's OK too. Be patient and keep on with the training.

Other Methods

There are lots of ways to meditate. You can meditate on a mantra or koan, you can do moving meditation or transcendental meditation, you can focus on a candle or all your surroundings, there's loving-kindness meditation and equanimity meditation, and much more.

We're not going to worry about all these methods for now. Our basic practice will be sitting meditation while bringing awareness first on the body, then the breath.

We will get into a few other practices in this book that I've found very useful, but always start with this basic practice during a meditation session before moving on to the new practice.

Exercise

Try the basic body awareness and breath awareness meditation now. Set a timer for two minutes, and try to notice your body and then your breath until the timer goes off. Don't worry about getting it perfect, just give it a shot and see what you learn, and where confusion comes up.

Chapter 3

THE 15 PROBLEMS YOU'LL FACE

As you start your meditation training, you'll notice that it's not as easy as you might have thought. You might be confused, worried you're doing it wrong, worried you're bad at it. That's completely normal.

Here's the way to look at it: we're not trying to get perfect at meditation. We're trying to learn to become aware of our mind wandering and what's coming up in our minds, and we're also trying to learn to deal with the struggles.

So when you're coming across these problems, that's good news! You're aware of the problems, and you have some good struggles to learn to deal with.

We'll talk about dealing with struggles in a bit but let's briefly look at some problems you might be facing as you meditate.

I'm going to give you some thoughts on each, just as reassurance that you're doing OK.

Lots of these are related or similar to each other:

1. Mind wanders all the time or thoughts keep coming up. This is normal! Everyone's mind does it. It's your mind's habit, and in fact your mind does this all the time. Meditation just helps you to bring awareness to it, because you're trying to focus on one object (your breath) and you can now see when your mind wanders away from that object. This awareness is what we're going after! So if you notice your mind wandering, you're successful. Keep at it, the wandering won't go away but you'll learn to be more patient with it.

2. Confused about how to do it. This is natural — anytime you start a new activity, you'll be confused about it. Allow yourself to feel the confusion, and stay with that feeling. It's really good to practice with!

3. Feeling like you're doing it wrong. Yep, everyone feels this way. You're not doing it wrong. There's no right way. Just showing up and staying with yourself is doing it right. So keep showing up. And when the feeling that you're doing it wrong comes up, stay with that. Practice with it.

4. Feeling like you suck at it. This, too, is a normal feeling. You don't suck at it, but everyone feels like they do, because you have difficulty keeping your attention on your breath, you get lost in thought, you get frustrated, and you don't feel as calm as you hoped you would be. So it's good to work with

this feeling too — see that you have some ideal that's causing you to feel bad about how you're doing, see that you are feeling disappointment, allow yourself to feel this. Stay with the feeling.

5. Not meditating consistently every day. This is also very common. You have the best of intentions, but you procrastinate or get busy and feel you can't do it right now. Or you start checking email and Facebook and never end up meditating. So it's normal, but the thing to become aware of is the moment when you turn away from your commitment to meditate and towards something that you have the urge to do (like check email or news). Notice the urge, notice the fear or desire that's driving the urge. If you do this, you are practicing. You might even sit with the urge for a few moments, just noticing it, just staying with it. After that, you might even feel like meditating for a minute longer.

6. Frustration arising. If you aren't as focused as you like to be, you might feel frustration. That's OK. Let yourself feel it. Notice how it feels. Stay with the feeling. Turn towards it with gentleness. We'll get into this practice, for dealing with all of these struggles, in a few chapters.

7. Difficult feelings coming up. You might experience fear or anger or depressing feelings as you sit in meditation. This is completely OK. Normally we want to run from these feelings, go do something else, so you might get the urge to get up and

avoid what you're feeling. Try not to get up, but just sit still, and face the feelings with courage. See how it feels. Notice that it's not a big deal. More on this in future chapters.

8. The urge to quit or check on email/social media. If you're sitting, you might want to get up before your timer is done. That's OK, but instead of getting up, sit for a moment or two longer, noticing the urge. The urge will probably go away after a bit. When the urge comes back, sit with it and don't get up. It will go away soon. When it comes back a third time, allow yourself to get up. This is finding the edge between working with discomfort and not overdoing it.

9. Disappointment that it's not bringing you peace and happiness. It would be great if we could cause ourselves to enter a perfect mental state and everything would be awesome. But this isn't reality. Sometimes you'll feel peace, sometimes happiness, but often other feelings will arise — boredom, agitation, tiredness, anxiety. There's no "right" way to feel during meditation. What we want is to develop the ability to let anything come up, any feeling, and just be with it.

10. Uncomfortable while you're sitting. Some physical discomfort is OK, but you don't want pain or extreme discomfort. If you're only meditating for a couple minutes, you might be sitting in an uncomfortable position and should try to find a better position and make sure you're relaxed. But

as you go longer, there will inevitably be some discomfort, and learning to deal with that struggle is a skill you can learn during meditation with practice.

11. Drowsiness. It's normal to start to nod off when you're meditating, especially if you're doing it early in the morning or at the end of a long, tiring day. Don't worry, there's nothing wrong with that. I try to wake myself up by blinking my eyes, stretching my face in various ways, even pinching myself in a loving way. Just notice your struggle and give yourself some compassion.

12. Boredom. We're so used to being busy, to getting lots of information from computers and phones, that sitting still and doing nothing can quickly bring on boredom. It's good to be aware of the mind's wanting to run from stillness, wanting to go check on things and do something more exciting. This is your mind's resistance to staying present. It's actually wonderful to develop awareness to this resistance, and sit and watch it arise in you. It goes away if you don't do anything but watch the resistance.

13. Resistance to meditation. You might have reluctance to meditate, you might actively dislike it, you might tell yourself reasons why it's stupid or not for you. This resistance is also quite common. Sit and watch your resistance, face it and feel it. It can feel like a hardness, like an aversion but explore it with curiosity and notice everything

you can about it. This sitting and noticing is meditation.

14. No time for meditation. Thinking that you have no time is actually a form of resistance to meditation (see item above). You have time even one or two minutes is all you need to do to practice. You just feel rushed, feel like there are other things to do. That's normal. And again, like the resistance above, you can sit still and face this feeling. Again, more about this process in future chapters.

15. Can't clear my mind of all thoughts. This isn't the goal of meditation. That's a misconception. Sometimes it does happen, but we're not shooting for that. Let that goal go, and instead allow whatever thoughts you have to arise, notice them, and be OK with them. They're just things that come up, like clouds or wind, and seeing or feeling them is a good thing to practice.

As you can see, all of these problems (and others) are quite normal. And they are useful places to direct your mindfulness practice. In truth, we face these kinds of problems all day, for all kinds of situations, not just meditation. And learning to become aware and deal mindfully with these problems is an incredible skill to develop. We'll work on all of this in upcoming chapters, but for now, just know that it's perfectly OK to have these problems, and they are part of the practice.

The 15 Problems You'll Face

Exercise

Sit for a minute and notice what resistance you've been feeling, what confusion, what disappointment, what difficulty you've had from meditation. Stay still with it, notice how it feels, and have to courage to face it with curiosity.

Chapter 4

How to Progress

OK, you've tried your first meditation or two (or perhaps you already knew how to do it) you might be wondering: what now?

It's one thing to sit and notice your body and breath for a couple minutes, it's quite another to really get good at mindfulness.

So two things to say about this:

First, toss out the idea of getting "good" at mindfulness. You might make progress, but at some level you'll always suck at it. I sure do. I know people who have been meditating for 30 years, even Zen priests, and they talk about their current struggles and not being "good" at it. Yet at another level, they're "good" because they keep doing it, and good because they've come to accept that they're never going to be close to "perfect" at it, whatever that means.

How to Progress

Next, you make progress one step at a time. One two-minute meditation session at a time. So set a daily reminder for yourself, and every day, sit and pay attention for just two minutes. This is how you make progress.

You'll struggle. Your mind will wander, you'll get bored, you'll want to get up, you'll miss a day or three, you'll feel like you're doing it wrong all the problems we discussed in the last chapter. This is how you make progress — by struggling and paying attention. Struggling and sitting still with it.

We're going to talk about the struggle in the next few chapters but for now, just know that this struggle is a part of the process, *the* way to make progress. You don't make progress without it. In fact, it is the heart of the practice itself — the struggle *is* the practice. Focusing on the breath is just the way to notice the struggle.

So sit every day, for a couple minutes a day.

You might want to lengthen your meditation to five minutes, or 10, or 20 or 30. That's normal, but resist this urge for now. Sit with the urge and watch it, become aware of it, don't act on it.

You can increase to five minutes after a week of doing it without missing. Don't let yourself increase to five minutes otherwise. After another week of doing it for five minutes without missing, increase to seven.

Then 10 minutes after another week. But if you miss even one day during a week, stay at your current level. If you miss a few days, drop back to the previous level. Actually, they're not "levels" but just durations. It really doesn't matter how long you meditate, as long as you keep doing it.

You'll notice progress after a while, because you'll get better at sitting still. You'll get better at noticing when your mind wanders (that's "when" not "if"). You'll start to become more aware of your resistance, your urges, your frustrations not only during meditation but at other times during the day.

The practice is always the sitting meditation, but you apply the practice to other parts of your life, eventually. We'll get to that, but just know that the dojo, the practice space, is always the sitting meditation.

And smile. Don't worry so much about making progress or getting good at it, but just smile and enjoy every sitting session. You're not on your way to somewhere amazing — you're already there.

Exercise

Simply sit in meditation for two minutes a day for the next few days. Don't get caught up in what comes next, how long this will take, whether you're doing it right, how hard it is. Just focus on your body, then your breath. Stay present as much as you can, and notice when you've wandered, gently returning to your breath.

Chapter 5

WORKING WITH YOUR STRUGGLE

As we've discussed, you might be struggling in meditation so far with uncertainty, discomfort, the urge to quit, disliking it.

This is exactly why we're here.

Through learning to work with our struggles in meditation, we'll create awareness of what's going on behind the scenes, and the skills to cope with these struggles for dealing with the same kinds of struggles we find throughout the day.

For example, these struggles we find in meditation are the same ones we find in everyday life that lead to procrastination, frustration, relationship problems, unhappiness and more:

- Uncertainty
- Fear
- Disappointment with our experiences

Working with Your Struggle 21

- Unhappiness with ourselves
- Frustration with how things are going
- Anxiety about how we're doing
- Worry about how we'll do in the future
- Stress about getting things right
- Negative self-talk
- A story we're telling ourselves about what we're doing

We don't often realize it, but these are present almost every moment of the day. Meditation just brings it all to light, and it's when it comes to light that we can actually work with this stuff.

How to Work with Struggles

See the struggle as your practice ground. In that way, it's awesome! You can't get better at it if you don't have something to practice with.

Now, if you see fear, uncertainty, disappointment, frustration, anxiety or other struggles come up here's how to start working with them:

1. Shine the light of awareness on the struggle. Turn towards it and see that it's there. Acknowledge it, as you would acknowledge a friend if she walked into the room.

2. Invite the struggle in. Smile and say hello to your struggle. Instead of running from the struggle like it's a hated enemy, warmly invite the struggle into the room as if you'd like to have tea with it, and a good conversation.

3. Stay with courage. Our normal way of dealing with difficulties is to not want them here, to avoid them, to distract ourselves. Instead, stay. Just keep your attention here and have the courage to stay.

4. Explore with curiosity. We often think we know that the difficulty is going to be horrible if we don't run from it. But how do we know? Pretend you know nothing about this struggle, and instead say, "Hmm, what's it like?" Throw out all preconceptions, and just be curious.

5. Feel it physically. Instead of having a vague idea about the struggle, or telling yourself a story about it, just feel it. How does it feel, physically, in your body? Where is it located? What kind of energy does it have? Does that shift over time?

6. Give it compassion. Imagine that this struggle were a friend of yours, instead of an enemy. If your friend were having difficulty, would you run from your friend? Would you avoid him? Would you be harsh and critical? Or would you be gentle, compassionate, loving? Extend a loving heart towards your struggle.

That's the process. It's not easy, and you won't master it in one try. In fact, you might struggle with it. If so, work with that!

Exercise

In your meditation today, sit and notice if you have any difficulty. Try the method above, or at least a few of the steps, with this struggle. In future meditations, whenever you notice frustration, fear, anxiety, uncertainty use this method. Review it daily until you have it memorized.

Chapter 6

WHY WE STRUGGLE

So what's the deal with all of these struggles we normally have? Why do we keep having them? Maybe if we could figure that out, we could solve them, right?

Well, I'm not sure we'll ever "solve" all of our struggles, but it is helpful to understand them. And in understanding, we can learn to work with them in a helpful way.

So let's take a look at what's going on

When we are frustrated with someone else, for example, this is what's happening:

1. We have an idea of how we think they should behave.

2. They behave differently than we'd like — we might call this "inconsiderate," or "irritating," or "wrong," but really it's just behavior that's different than what we'd like.

Why We Struggle

3. The difference between reality (how they're behaving) and our ideal is what causes frustration.

This is also what causes anger, disappointment, and hurt feelings. There's an ideal, reality doesn't meet our ideal, and we become frustrated, hurt, disappointed, angry.

But what about fear, uncertainty, anxiety? What about unhappiness with ourselves? These also come from pretty much the same source: the difference between our ideals and reality.

Fear, Anxiety and Uncertainty

Fear, anxiety and uncertainty are really all the same thing (with different names):

We don't know how the future will turn out. We don't know whether we'll be OK. We are uncertain about how things will go, how we'll do, how others will react. And we fear this uncertainty.

Fear of failure, fear of looking dumb, fear of some scary situation, is all really just fear of uncertainty about the future.

So let's look at the process of fear of uncertainty:

1. We would like things to be safe, certain, under control, familiar, comfortable. This is our ideal for life, even if we don't realize it, admit it to

ourselves, it's what we want: certainty, control and comfort.

2. Life is never ever certain. It's often uncomfortable. It's never really under our control. So it doesn't meet with our ideal.

3. The difference between reality (uncertain, uncomfortable, uncontrollable) and our ideal causes the stress and fear.

Again, reality isn't meeting our ideal, and it causes stress and fear and discomfort.

Unfortunately, life is never certain, controllable, or ideal. It's often difficult and uncomfortable. And so, very often, difficulty and struggle arises.

How to Handle This Difficulty

Looking at it with this perspective, we can see that we only really have two choices:

1. Change life to fit our ideals. That means try to make other people act the way we want them to (or believe they should), make life under our control, always have comfort and certainty, make everything in our lives perfect. Lots of people actually try this, but I've not found it to be possible. You can create every system in the world, and get everything in order, and you'll find that it's all an illusion.

2. Loosen up on our ideals. If life won't fit our ideals, and that's causing us so many problems how about if we let go of the ideals? Or at least not hold so tightly to them. Unfortunately this is not so easy — we really want our ideals to become reality! We want everyone (including ourselves) to behave ideally. We want the world to go according to plan. Letting go of these ideals is much easier said than done.

You could also just continue to struggle. Or run from the struggles, avoiding them and distracting yourself and trying to comfort your pain with food and shopping and alcohol and TV and social media and video games and drugs. Yes, this is very common — and in fact, it's a version of #1 above, trying to get life to be more comfortable and less difficult. It doesn't work very well, because we're just running from our problems, scratching our itches, making everything worse in the long run.

The answer is to loosen our attachment to ideals. It's what we'll work on with mindfulness practice.

Exercise

As you meditate today, reflect on what struggles you've had, and how these struggles are a result of life (including other people) not meeting your ideals.

How easy would it be to let go of these ideals? Try it and find out!

Chapter 7

The Heart of the Struggle Is Groundlessness

In the last chapter, we talked about why we struggle: attachment to our ideals, and life not meeting our ideals. The answer seems easy — just let go of those ideals, right? But in truth, we cling. We get caught up.

Why do we cling so much to these ideals of how things should be, to the ideals of comfort and control?

For one thing, it's very scary when things are out of control, chaotic, slipping away from us. It's painful when we suffer a loss, when things change suddenly and dramatically and we can't do anything about it.

Think about the times when life was turned upside down: when you lost a job, lost a loved one, became ill, suffered a crisis. Maybe you went through a natural disaster, were told that a loved one had a fatal disease, lost a home.

How did this feel? It felt like the ground was pulled from under you, like you had nothing solid under your feet. You thought you had solid ground, but then everything you thought was solid all of a sudden wasn't. This is extremely disrupting, disconcerting, upending, frightening.

The human mind doesn't like this loss of control. And yet, it happens all the time — not just when major life disruptions and losses happen, but every day. When something happens to cause discomfort, when you receive difficult news, when plans are suddenly changed, when someone interrupts you these and many other everyday things that happen to us are all minor versions of the ground being pulled from under our feet.

When we experience what Buddhist teacher Pema Chödrön calls "groundlessness," we experience fear and pain. And we immediately try to reach for solid ground. Some of the ways we try to get solid ground include:

- Clinging to an ideal even if the ideal isn't real.

- Trying to regain control by ordering people around, making a plan, creating an orderly list, making a system.

- Avoiding the pain and finding something comfortable or pleasurable — food, alcohol, drugs, shopping, TV, video games, the Internet. Procrastination is one form of this.

- Getting mad at someone. Striking out at them.

In fact, there are a million ways we try to reach for solid ground, when we feel groundlessness. It actually takes up most of our day.

What would happen if, instead of scrambling for solid ground in one of our million habitual ways, we just accepted the groundlessness?

What if we just sat with the feeling of groundlessness? What if we just stayed with the feelings of fear and loss and pain and loss of control?

What if we learned to become OK with this feeling of groundlessness? Even comfortable with it?

This is what we're doing when we practice mindfulness. Meditation is a constant practice of staying with the groundlessness.

How so? Think about what we're practicing with in meditation:

- We try to focus on the breath and fail, so we deal with the groundlessness of failure and frustration.

- We are constantly unsure of whether we're doing it right, so we're facing the groundlessness of uncertainty and self-doubt.

- We face our frustrations and attachments that stem from everyday life situations, instead of avoiding them. We sit with the groundlessness of those situations, when normally we'll run from them towards distraction and comfort.

- We face the physical discomfort we might feel from sitting, or the discomfort of boredom.

- We might face the urge to quit or go do something else like check email, and the discomfort that follows from not following that urge.

The list could go on, but you can see that in many ways, meditation is really practice in staying with groundlessness.

So if you're feeling groundlessness when you meditate, that's exactly what you should be feeling. It's what we feel in various ways throughout the day, but we run from this feeling of groundlessness, we go to distraction or try to gain control. In meditation, we face it. We stay, with courage and curiosity.

We learn to become comfortable with this groundlessness, and in doing so we begin to build trust in ourselves that we can be OK whenever groundlessness arises in its thousands of forms.

Exercise

As you sit in meditation today, notice when you feel groundlessness, and just sit with it. Just face it and see what it's like. Notice that it's not a big deal to feel it, and the world doesn't fall apart if you stay with it.

Chapter 8

STAYING WITH CURIOSITY AND COMPASSION

Very few of us realize we're doing it, but our habitual response to fear, discomfort, frustration, uncertainty is to run.

We do everything we can to avoid difficult feelings:

- We go to distraction or comfort ourselves
- We try to get things under control by planning and creating systems
- We complain, get angry, cry, anything but actually facing the feeling

We have lots of ways to avoid these feelings. We do them without thinking. It's how we get so trapped in procrastination and debt and clutter, for example. Avoidance takes up most of our day, most days.

So avoiding these feelings is not helpful, and ends up taking up a lot of our energy and time

What can we do instead? I think you know what my answer is: stay with the feeling.

When you notice yourself wanting to run stay.

Think of your mind like it's a little puppy train it to stay, with gentleness.

Learning to Be a Friend to Yourself

Think about how often we turn away from whatever is arising in us — how would you feel if a good friend always avoided you when you had difficulty? It would feel like you were unwanted, and that wouldn't be a good friend. A good friend stays.

So just as you would stay and listen to a good friend who is struggle, stay and pay attention to yourself when you're struggling. Have compassion for yourself, try to understand what you're going through, and most importantly, just be there.

How? We are training the mind to stay when we meditate: instead of running from the present moment, from whatever arises, we sit still and pay attention.

So as you meditate, try this:

- Notice when you're frustrated, angry, fearful, uncertain.

- Notice the urge to run from this.

- Instead, turn towards the feeling. Tell your mind to stay, with gentleness, not harshness. Find the courage to stay.

- Try to be curious about the feeling, instead of already knowing that it will "suck." What is it like? Where is the feeling located? What can you learn about it?

- Notice that it's not that big a deal. You are OK. It's uncomfortable, but not the end of the world.

This is the practice. Continue to work with this, with courage, with curiosity. You can do this!

As you practice, you'll get better over time. Not "perfect," but more trusting in yourself to stay. More accepting of whatever is arising for you.

You'll also learn to practice this in your everyday life, not just meditation. This is where you'll see some great benefits, because you'll learn that you can stay with your feeling without needing to run, without needing to act on it, without needing to control the situation. You just sit and watch, and have the feeling that it will be OK.

This is an incredible step, because now you don't need to avoid anymore. This helps you with procrastination, forming new habits, becoming healthy, learning to stay present instead of running to distraction. You won't be perfect at this, but you'll learn that you

Staying with Curiosity and Compassion

don't need all of that distraction and avoidance. You can be OK without it.

Exercise

As you meditate, practice the steps above. Try it every day — stay with whatever arises, with courage and curiosity.

Chapter 9

How to Not Cling

We talked about the idea of loosening our attachment to ideals but it's easier said than done. We tend to cling to these ideals, and knowing that we're clinging is only the first step.

The problem is that we often don't want to loosen our attachments to ideals. No, what we really want is for the ideals to come true. That's because we're clinging tightly!

So how do we get around this problem? How do we deal with tight clinging?

There's a mindfulness practice that can help us work with this clinging. It's called compassion practice.

Here's how you do it:

- Sit in meditation, and think of someone you love wholeheartedly, in an uncomplicated way. We tend to have more complex feelings about parents and spouses, so if that's the case for you, try something simpler — perhaps a child or really good friend.

- Think about this person, and imagine them in pain or struggling with something.
- Find a place in your heart to *wish for their struggle or pain to end*. Wish for them to be free of pain, free of struggle, free of any kind of suffering.
- Notice the place in your heart where compassion comes out.

Now repeat this exercise with another friend or family member. Now try it by thinking of a neighbor or co-worker who you don't know well. Now imagine a stranger you meet on the street, and do the practice.

What you're cultivating is the practice of compassion. It's a useful skill for all kinds of things, including our own clinging.

Using Compassion on Clinging

Practice the compassion exercise above a few times in meditation before trying it on your own clinging. It's helpful to see the place in your heart where compassion emerges.

Now, when you sit in meditation, if you notice yourself clinging to an ideal (examples: meditating perfectly, wanting to be comfortable) try this:

- Notice that you're clinging to an ideal. If you can let it go immediately, great!

- If you're still clinging, notice the stress that results from that clinging.

- Give yourself compassion. From the same place in your heart, wish for your stress and difficulty with this clinging to be over. Give your stress some love.

- Notice if this loosens your clinging at all. It might not completely dissolve it, but it can allow you to be in a place where you don't need the ideal so much.

Practice this a many times as you can in meditation. It's incredibly helpful in everyday life.

Exercise

Spend a few days working with the compassion practice outlined above.

Chapter 10

DEVELOPING PATIENCE

Who among us possesses a saintlike patience? Very few of us, if we're honest with ourselves. We get frustrated with other people, with everyday situations, with ourselves.

I know in my life, if I'm reading or trying to focus on work, and my wife or kids interrupts me, I lose patience very quickly. A frustration just pops up out of nowhere, and I forget my love for them and just want them not to disturb me!

We see this impatience all the time in ourselves, and in others. And it causes harm — it can hurt other people who just want our attention, it can hurt our relationship with people we care about, it can even harm our professional relationships and therefore our careers.

So what can be done? There's a practice similar to the compassion exercise we tried in the last chapter, that I've found helpful when I'm frustrated or losing patience. It's called "loving-kindness practice."

It's very similar to compassion practice — here's how you do it:

- Sit in meditation, and think of someone you love wholeheartedly, in an uncomplicated way — perhaps a child or really good friend.

- Think about this person, think to yourself, "May they be happy." Simply wish for their happiness, from a place in your heart.

- Notice the place in your heart where this loving kindness comes from.

Again, you should repeat this exercise with another friend or family member. Now try it by thinking of a neighbor or co-worker who you don't know well. Now imagine a stranger you meet on the street, and do the practice.

What's the point of this? You're cultivating loving-kindness, which can be used when you're losing patience.

A Patience Practice

Try this when you're losing patience:

- Notice that you're frustrated or feeling impatient.

Developing Patience

- Notice the stress that you feel as a result of clinging to the way you want things to be.
- Give yourself some loving-kindness. Simply wish for yourself to be happy.
- Do the same for the other person, who you're losing patience with.

I also find it useful to try to practice gratitude towards that other person — why am I grateful to have them in my life? It's easy to focus on the inconsiderate thing they're doing, but what good qualities do they have? How can I see the loving heart they have in themselves?

Exercise

As you sit in meditation, practice the loving-kindness exercise outlined above. Try it while thinking about other people, including strangers, and when thinking about yourself.

Chapter 11

DEALING WITH OVERWHELM

Who among us doesn't get overwhelmed by life sometimes? Or perhaps every day, by the chaos of work and everything going on around us?

Being overwhelmed can lead to stress and unhappiness with life but it's not completely necessary. Given the same external situation, you can either react by feeling overwhelmed and full of anxiety or you can respond with equanimity and calm.

Yes, it's easier said than done. When everything seems to be coming at you at once, or you feel overloaded with too much to do it's not so easy to find peace in the middle of the chaos.

So how do we learn to deal with everything more peacefully? There's a practice that is called "equanimity practice" that can be helpful.

It's similar to the compassion and loving-kindness practices — here's how you do it:

Dealing with Overwhelm

- Sit in meditation, and look around you at everything you can see. Try to take in everything around you, without focusing on any one thing. Just notice the shapes and colors of everything.

- Now try to notice all sounds around you, within the room and outside of it.

- Now take in all sounds and sights at once, just soaking in all the sensations of the world around you. Include yourself in this field of awareness.

- Finally, try to emanate love to everything around you. Feel love for everything equally, radiating it in all directions.

- Expand this love to include everything in the world, in all directions, including all people.

This is a feeling of equanimity, loving everything equally. Everything around you, including any people around you, including yourself. Including the entire universe.

It can be cultivated with practice in meditation, and when you're feeling overwhelmed, you can use equanimity to realize that you're in the middle of joy and beauty.

Try it like this: as you become overwhelmed and stressed, pause. Take a breath. Notice the feeling of being overwhelmed. Stay with that feeling. Now try equanimity practice — see everything around you, including the things and people who are making you stressed or overwhelmed, and send a feeling of love to all of them.

This can calm you down and make you feel better about your situation. It can help you to realize that while it's easy to be unhappy about everything around you, it's also possible to be grateful for them, to love them and feel compassion towards them. And in this shift, it can transform how you feel about everything and your relationship with those around you.

I'm not saying this is always easy, or even possible all the time. But this is a helpful practice, and I encourage you to try it when you're feeling overwhelmed.

Exercise

In your next few meditation sessions, practice the equanimity exercise I outline above. Cultivate this ability, because it can be useful at any moment in your life.

Chapter 12

Changing Habits

The steps for changing a habit are fairly simple, from a mechanical point of view:

1. Pick a habit and start small, with the tiniest iteration of it (one pushup, two minutes meditating, etc.).

2. Pick a trigger — something you already do in your regular life, like waking up or brushing your teeth or opening your laptop. You're going to try to do the habit right after this, making the trigger-habit combo automatic after a bunch of repetitions.

3. Set reminders so you remember to do the habit right after the trigger. Visual reminders are helpful, like a post-it note near the trigger.

4. Do the habit after the trigger for at least a month. Six weeks is even better. It will become more and more automatic.

5. Get accountability for when you don't feel like doing it.

Those five steps are all it takes. Add more accountability if things start to falter. Otherwise, it's a pretty simple process.

So why is it so difficult for most people? It's not because the steps are hard. It's because they feel resistance.

The Resistance

We all feel resistance to doing things sometimes. Often it's because of one or more of these reasons:

1. Doing the action is uncomfortable.

2. We have a story in our heads (I call it a "Mind Movie") about what's going on in our lives right now, and the current story is stopping us. For example, we might have a story about how hard life is, about how we hate exercise or vegetables, about how we suck at sticking to habits. This story can get in the way of action.

3. Our self talk is negative. We're always talking to ourselves, even if we're not aware of it. For example, we might think, "This is too hard," or "I deserve a break," or "I'll do it later, I'm tired right now."

These three reasons are actually all related, but they're different ways of looking at the resistance. Usually, they're all happening at once. And they might not be such a big deal, but in small ways, they can sabotage habits and other attempts at positive changes.

Dealing with the Resistance

How can we overcome the resistance that we often face, that gets in the way of forming habits (and taking other positive steps)? You might be shocked to know that the answer starts with mindfulness. Actually, you can't really make good changes in your life without mindfulness, I've found.

Here's the method I recommend:

- Notice the resistance. Shine the spotlight of awareness on the feeling of not wanting to do your new habit. The same is true of procrastination. It's a feeling of wanting to avoid, wanting to run to distraction.

- Notice your story and self-talk. What movie is playing in your mind about the action you're supposed to take? What are you telling yourself about this action, about your current situation? You might not be able to tell, but it's good to try to notice what's going on if possible.

- Drop below the story, and stay with the feeling.

The story you're telling yourself is causing the resistance. That's going on in your head. Try dropping below the story in your head, down to the feeling in your body beneath the story. How does it feel physically? Stay with this feeling, with courage and curiosity, as you've been practicing.

- Remember your intention. What's your deeper reason for wanting to take this action? If it's just because you think it would "be nice," then you won't have the motivation to push through. Instead, do the habit out of compassion for yourself, for other people who are important to you, or for the world. Do it out of love. Remember this as you prepare to overcome the resistance.

- Take a small action, out of love. Do the smallest possible step, and do it with love for whoever will benefit from your habit change. For example, when I felt resistance to running, I told myself I just had to put on my shoes and get out the door. That's so easy, it felt ridiculous *not* doing it. And if you're doing it out of love for yourself, or to set a good example with love for others it becomes an easy choice.

- Forgive yourself when you mess up. You're not going to be perfect at this, so it's good to practice letting go of your expectations of being awesome at it. Instead, forgive yourself for whatever transgressions you've made, and let that go. Otherwise, bad feelings about messing up will only stand in your way.

Changing Habits

Yes, I know it's easier to write this out than to actually put it into practice. That's why we practice, and why we forgive ourselves when we mess up.

Exercise

You've likely already encountered resistance to meditation — not wanting to sit on some days. This is good, it's a rich area to work with! The next time you feel resistance to meditating, stop and practice the method above. You can also try it with any kind of procrastination, any kind of habit you're trying to stick to, such as exercise. Practice!

Chapter 13

FINDING FOCUS

Procrastination is such a common problem that I believe it's universal. And it can get so that you're spending entire days running from difficult tasks, spending your life in distraction and avoidance.

Whether you've gotten to this extreme or not, it's a useful mindfulness practice to work with the urges that come up that cause us to procrastinate.

Let's first look at what happens when we procrastinate:

1. The prospect of starting or sticking to a difficult task seems uncomfortable. It's hard, overwhelming, scary, full of uncertainty.

2. So your mind immediately has the urge to run. Run to distractions, run to cleaning up, run to doing any kind of busywork but the difficult, uncomfortable task.

Finding Focus

3. You follow the urge out of habitual conditioning.

There isn't really anything you can do about the first two steps on this list. Your mind will feel discomfort when faced with difficulty, uncertainty, fear, feeling overwhelmed. You will have the urge to run. You don't control your mind to the degree where you can prevent yourself feeling discomfort, fear, or urges.

However, you can change the habit of following the urge to run. This is not completely under your control, as you won't be able to be aware of the urge 100% of the time. And sometimes, even aware of the urge, you'll still follow it.

But you can learn not to follow *every* urge.

Here's how to work with urges:

- Create a practice space — have one important task that you're going to focus on for five minutes. Clear everything away and just have you and that task, nothing else.

- Set a timer, do nothing but the task. Your choices are to do the task, or sit there doing nothing. Set the time for five minutes.

- Watch the urge to switch away from the task. You'll very likely have the urge to go do something else, check email, check the news, check your favorite distractions, clean up, anything but stay with the task. This is good! Watch the urge.

- Face the urge and stay with it. Don't actually run from the task, but instead just face the urge. See what you can discover about it. Watch it rise, then fall. Notice its energy.

- See that there's no big deal. You can stay with the urge, not follow it, just watch it and the world doesn't fall apart! It's not a reason to panic. In fact, it's no big deal.

- Return to focusing on the task. The urge to switch passes, return to the task with love. You'll feel fear, uncertainty, discomfort and that's OK. You'll be perfectly fine.

This is a powerful practice, creating a practice space and staying with the urge without acting on it. Try it! You might find that you're capable of more than you have guessed.

Exercise

You can do this focus practice instead of meditation today, or in addition to it. Just five minutes! Try it for a few days at least. It's a useful practice to work on every day, actually.

Chapter 14

HOW TO GET BETTER

We've covered the basics of mindfulness — in fact, we've gone beyond the very beginner skills to some intermediate practices. I just like to deliver more than I promise. :)

The basics are to learn simple sitting meditation, and to work with whatever struggles arise with courage, curiosity, and gentleness. Adding compassion is a great bonus!

The question is how to take what you've read and put it into practice. How to get better at the skills you're struggling with.

I have three suggestions.

First: Practice Nearly Daily

A short daily practice is so much more effective than just reading a book. I can't recommend it highly enough

— if you really want to get your money's worth with this book, the most important thing you can do is practice every day.

It doesn't have to be long: keep doing just two minutes a day. After that gets way too easy and you're pretty consistent, feel free to stretch it to five minutes. But don't be in a rush — it's more important to do it consistently than it is to lengthen the duration. Gradually work your way to 10 minutes, then 15, if you like. The length doesn't matter much.

I say practice daily, but the reality is that most of us miss a day or two now and then. That's OK. If you miss more, that's OK too. Just start right back up again. And keep going! The more you practice, the more you'll really get this.

Second: Review the Exercises

Go back over the exercises in the preceding chapters and try them again and again. You'll get more out of them as you revisit them — that's what I've found, at least.

Start with the basic body and breath practice every day, but then try the other practices we discussed. Mix it up — you can work with one for a week, then another, or you can rotate through them every day, or even do two in a day if you feel like it. It doesn't matter much. Some of you will want a definite practice plan, but I'm not going to give you that certainty — work with the uncertainty!

Practice these exercises outside of meditation as well. Do them in your daily life as you encounter frustration, stress, fear, anger, uncertainty, resistance. Go back and read the relevant chapter, and work with them. Soon you won't need to read the chapter, you'll just know what to practice when you encounter something.

Third: Work with Whatever Arises

In your life, different things will come up. You'll get in a fight with a loved one, get frustrated with a co-worker, be disappointed with yourself, procrastinate, struggle with habits, stop meditating and face resistance, encounter many different fears and irritations, and much more.

This is what you should work with. Whatever comes up, that's your practice ground. You'll always have material to practice with. That's what life is about — it is constantly throwing something at you.

Whatever comes up, find one of the exercises and practice with it.

See every single thing, every person, every moment,

as a teacher. When you find something or someone frustrates you, thank the universe for giving you a great teacher!

In the End

This book wasn't meant to have you master all these ideas in one shot. That's impossible. Instead, we wanted to dive in and start working with the basic mindfulness practices, get dirty and mess things up, and in the end learn a lot about these ideas and about ourselves.

Have you been able to sit in meditation, at least a few times? Congratulations! That's an amazing step towards learning these mindfulness concepts.

Have you been able to practice any of the exercises in this book? That's another amazing achievement.

Can you stop right now, and appreciate the greatness of this moment? I'm glad — that makes me happy, because I wrote this book with your happiness in mind. Thanks for paying attention.

About the Author

Leo Babauta is the creator of Zen Habits, and author of the *Zen Habits* book as well as *Essential Zen Habits*. He has helped thousands of people change their habits, simplify their lives and practice mindfulness through his blog and his Sea Change membership program. He lives in Davis, California with his wife and six kids (several of whom are now adults!). He's a vegan, and enjoys running, reading, meditating, lifting weights and hiking.

Printed in the USA
CPSIA information can be obtained
at www.ICGtesting.com
LVHW020640311223
767624LV00082B/2921